DATE DUE

APR 22 1997		
Nov 06 02		
NO 15 '02		
JA 30 '04		
JA 27 '05		
AP 19 '05		
OC 17 '05		
NO 21 '06		
DE 20 '06		
AP 17 '07		
FEB 2 1 '08		
OCT 2 6 '10		
GAYLORD		PRINTED IN U S A

Military Aircraft Library
Spy Planes

Military Aircraft Library
Spy Planes

DR. DAVID BAKER

Rourke Enterprises, Inc.
Vero Beach, FL 32964

SPY PLANES

The Lockheed SR-71 developed in the early 1960s is still the most effective air reconnaissance plane in the world today and is capable of flying at more than three times the speed of sound.

Library of Congress Cataloging-in-Publication Data

Baker, David, 1944-
    Spy planes.

    (Military aircraft library)
    Includes index.
    Summary: Discusses the history of surveillance from the sky and describes the development of different types of reconnaissance aircraft and their uses since World War II.
    1. Reconnaissance aircraft—United States—Juvenile literature. [1. Reconnaissance aircraft. 2. Airplanes, Military] I. Title. II. Series: Baker, David, 1944-   . Military planes.
UG1242.R4B35 1987   358.4'5'0973   87-14141
ISBN 0-86592-353-1

CONTENTS

Spying from the Sky

Even before the world's first fighter took to the air, pilots were climbing into planes made of wood and canvas to spy on enemy troops. In fact, long before the first airplanes appeared at the beginning of this century, balloons and airships were regularly used to look out for enemy soldiers. Both sides in the American Civil War used balloons for spying, as did several countries during the nineteenth century. Reconnaissance, as it was called, helped bring about a revolution in tactical planning. For the first time, generals could plan their battles with reasonably accurate information about the state of the enemy and his positions.

When powered flight came along, armies acquired planes to do the job balloons had done. When the First World War broke out in Europe in 1914, a modest effort went into building up air forces to help provide detailed information

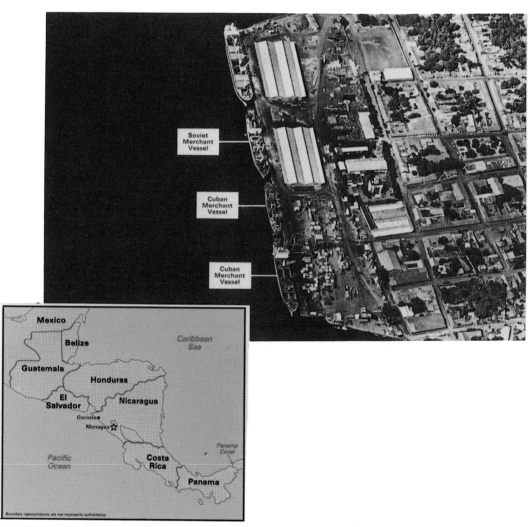

High altitude reconnaissance pictures have proven invaluable during peace time in gathering important information about neighboring countries, in this case merchant fleet operations in Nicaragua.

On the other side of the world, the Soviet build up of naval activity at the Vietnamese port of Cam Ranh Bay is clearly seen in these two aerial reconnaissance views.

about activities over on the other side. The war soon became one fought from trenches, with millions of soldiers fighting across the land between the miles of barbed wire that separated troop positions. Aerial reconnaissance became an increasingly important part of strategy. It very quickly became necessary to shoot down the enemy's reconnaissance planes, and guns fitted to ordinary aircraft gave birth to the concept of the fighter.

Meanwhile, crude attempts were made to improve reconnaissance planes, and aircraft were fitted with radio sets permitting the observer to talk to the ground and report what he saw. For spying on ships at sea, the Germans used airships, which differed from balloons in that they used hydrogen rather than heated air for lift. Most reconnaissance planes were equipped with box cameras slung over the side of the cockpit. Most carried guns with which to defend themselves from attacking fighters. By the end of the war in 1918 great progress had been made, both with reconnaissance planes and with fighters to attack them.

Not much improvement was made in reconnaissance equipment between the end of the First World War in 1918 and the beginning of the Second World War in 1939. When the Second World War ended in 1945, the field of science and technology was poised to make great forward leaps. Within twenty years a network of spy satellites ringed the globe, and jet fighters were modified to carry cameras at supersonic speed across the battlefield. It is a measure of the importance placed on reconnaissance that the most advanced military plane in the world today is not a fighter, nor a bomber, but an unarmed spy plane. Capable of flying at more than three times the speed of sound, the Lockheed SR-71 is used regularly to keep watch on movements in unfriendly countries.

The U-2 spy plane provided the United States with surveillance of potentially hostile countries during a critical period in the late 1950s when international tension brought a high demand for good information about foreign countries.

The Air Force used camouflaged versions of the U-2 on certain missions when high-flying jets began to challenge their activities.

MISSILE TRANSPORTERS

HEAVY EQUIPMENT

12 PROB GUIDELINE MISSILES

5 MISSILE DOLLIES

20' LONG CYLINDRICAL TANKS

MISSILE TRANSPORTERS

OPEN STORAGE

One of the most famous events of the 1960s was the detection by United States recon-naissance planes of a Soviet missile build up in Cuba.

Lower down the scale of sophistication, modified Phantom jets are equipped with sophisticated sensors for quickly gathering detailed information across wide geographics areas in time of war. In the last twenty years, sophisticated infrared scanners and powerful radar equipment have been developed to give battle commanders a full and complete file of detailed information about troop movements day and night. In peacetime, readiness to respond to surprise attack is maintained by the detailed radar images obtained by high flying TR-1 spy planes that "see" several hundred miles inside foreign territory, day or night and in clear weather or foul.

Since the Second World War, the United States has several times responded in time to save a major military confrontation because it maintains a close watch on suspicious activity around the world. Reconnaissance pictures obtained from high flying planes warned President John F. Kennedy in 1961 that Soviet premier Nikita Khrushchev was shipping long-range missiles to Cuba. The President was able to stop these ships and negotiate their return. In this way, information obtained well ahead of disputes that have the potential to flare into conflict helps maintain a stable peace. Such results make the seemingly unglamorous job of the reconnaissance pilot profoundly important.

Surveillance

Many wars have started because one side did not know what the other was doing. Still more have started because neither side could take steps to build up the right kind of defense at the right time. Too much military build-up leads to hostile countries becoming aggressive because they feel threatened. Too little build-up tempts the aggressor to take a chance and attack, thinking he can overwhelm a country he believes to be weaker. History is full of such examples. In trying to avoid such errors in the future, military planners and defense strategists try to gather as

Development of the U-2 led eventually to a redesigned version known as the TR-1, seen here in this magnificent high altitude view.

much information as possible about potentially hostile countries. In this way they hope to avoid being surprised or being perceived as a threat.

Surveillance is a form of investigation by legal means of things going on in a foreign country. It is a process of keeping watch on activities carried out beyond national boundaries. Surveillance is especially important in peacetime because it gives political leaders firm information and reduces the possibility of error in estimating the strength of a potential enemy. This can help leaders make the right decisions. When a Lockheed U-2 spy plane took pictures in 1962 of Soviet missile sites in Cuba, President Kennedy was able to rebut denials by Russian leader Nikita Khrushchev by showing him the photographs.

The U-2 was designed to fly very high and escape attack from hostile anti-aircraft missiles fired in an attempt to prevent pictures being taken of military installations. When the U-2 first appeared in 1955 it had a range of 2,200 miles and could reach a height of 70,000 feet. Soon, improvements were made which took the U-2 to a height of 85,000 feet, allowing it to fly more than 3,000 miles at a sedate 460 MPH. Aircraft of this type did much to help United States intelligence experts understand the range of technical developments under way in countries who closed their borders to the free exchange of

The Lockheed TR-1 is built for comparatively slow but very high flight, attaining altitudes well in excess of 70,000 feet carrying a variety of sensors and cameras.

information. It helped the United States match potential threats from many different areas around the world, thereby preserving a balance.

Most U-2s were equipped with simple black-and-white film cameras weighing 450 pounds. Each plane carried more than 2 miles of film, wound up in canisters, capable of shooting a strip below the plane 745 miles wide. This would have been sufficient to cover the United States on just twelve flights. Satellites eventually replaced the U-2 as a surveillance plane. For almost twenty years, U-2 flights were made for purely scientific reasons, taking advantage of the plane's great height and range capability. Then, in 1981, the air force took delivery of the latest development in this historic line.

Called the TR-1, it looked quite a lot like the U-2 but was much better equipped. Unlike its

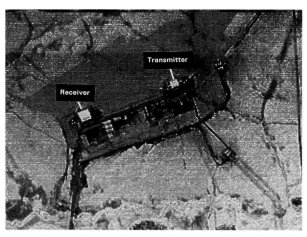

At one time photos like this of Soviet military installations might have been taken from high flying planes, but today satellites have replaced the U-2 for flights across Soviet air space.

A TR-1B trainer for the Lockheed-built surveillance plane operated by pilots of the 9th Strategic Reconnaissance Wing at Beale Air Force Base in Northern California.

predecessor, it could carry a wide range of optical and electronic sensors weighing a total 4,000 pounds, and its performance was greatly improved. With the ability to reach a height of more than 90,000 feet and fly 4,000 miles without refueling, the TR-1 could stay in the air for up to twelve hours. In its new role, the plane can electronically monitor events on the ground up to 360 miles either side of its flight path. That means it will sweep signals up from a strip 720 miles across as it flies along.

When using a special radar, it can "see" what is going on along the ground up to 58 miles either side, through rain or cloud, night or day. These radar images produce pictures made by reflected radio waves bouncing off objects on the ground. It enables intelligence experts to keep track of tanks, guns, artillery and large concentrations of troops. In that way, surprise would be more difficult to achieve. The TR-1 is kept busy monitoring activity in potential trouble spots. For instance, planes of this type fly from bases in England and West Germany and continually watch what is going on in East European countries. Although flying in West European air-space, the side looking radars and optical equipment keep watch nevertheless.

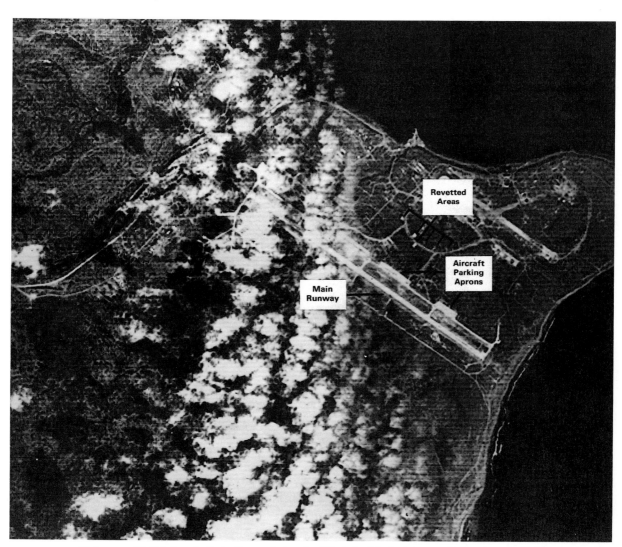

Pictures with this level of clarity are taken by TR-1, in this instance activity at an air field.

High Flight

Sometime in 1958 Lockheed began development of what is still the world's most remarkable airplane. It is the SR-71 Blackbird, so called because of its very deep blue, almost black, finish. The advent of anti-aircraft missiles called for newly designed reconnaissance planes. Conventional planes would not survive very long if

Pride of the Air Force's high altitude Mach 3 global surveillance capability is this Lockheed SR-71 Blackbird.

The SR-71 is made of special metals to protect it from excess heat at three times the speed of sound. Notice the unusual kinks and moldings in its delta-shaped wing.

attacked. Because the U-2 surveillance plane was too slow to outrun a fast flying missile, the team that built it put new efforts into designing its successor. At least, that was what it was supposed to be. As it turned out, both the slow flying U-2 and the fast flying SR-71 would see more than thirty years service together, although in different roles.

The SR-71 was built to conduct a high speed dash across enemy territory, gathering intelligence information as it went. In peacetime, it was to carry out important reconnaissance work with cameras and other sensors. The information it gathered would be vital to understanding military or political moves going on in a potentially unfriendly country. Above all, it had to survive. Its design provided it with only one means of survival: to fly very high and very fast.

Lockheed went to extraordinary trouble to make sure the Blackbird was faster than anything outside the United States. More than 35 years after it first took off in April, 1962, the SR-71 is still the fastest plane around.

The Blackbird's performance was shown publicly during a blistering sequence of record-breaking flights on two days in July, 1976. An SR-71 set a hot pace over 621 miles, averaging 2,092 MPH. The following day another SR-71 set a level-flight height record by cruising more than 85,000 feet above the earth, followed by another record the same day when a maximum speed of 2,193 MPH (Mach 3.3) was achieved. Two spectacular flights had taken place the year before. One plane made it from New York to London, England, in 1 hour and 56 minutes, and on the way back flew from London to Los Angeles, a

distance of 5,645 miles, in 3 hours and 47 minutes!

For the sake of high speed, the Blackbird is built very differently from conventional planes. The metals expand as the plane gets hotter. To allow room for this expansion without buckling, fuel leaks out before the plane takes off and warms up. Fortunately, the fuel is a special type that burns only under extremely high tempera-

The Blackbird has been used extensively to obtain intelligence information of use to politicians in peace time and have on several occasions provided details which help to relieve international crises.

The two pilots that fly the Blackbird sit in tandem seats, one behind the other, with the rear seat crew member responsible for operating the many sensors and cameras this plane can carry.

tures. In full flight the wings heat up to 500° F, twice as hot as a kitchen oven, while the rear engine parts are 1,100° F and glow a bright orange-white. To further help the airframe survive these temperatures, more than 93 percent of the structure is made from a special metal, titanium. Very resistant to corrosion, titanium is a white metal that melts at around 3,000° F. Titanium is a very expensive but vital solution to the problems caused by high speed.

The SR-71 has two crewmembers: a pilot in front and his systems operator behind. Each wears a special suit so advanced in design that astronauts used them on the first four NASA Shuttle flights during the period from 1981 to 1983. Behind the two crewmembers is an in-flight refueling port into which a tanker can insert a probe and top up the tanks. Almost the entire body of the plane and the wings out to the engines contain fuel that helps absorb some of the heat from friction with the air. Elsewhere on the plane, special sensors and cameras record information as the pilot flies while navigating with instruments that record star positions. At more than 85,000 feet, the sky can be very clear and star navigation is made easy.

On a typical mission, the SR-71 would fly from its base in the United States and rendezvous with a tanker, perhaps high above the Mediterranean Sea. Fully fueled, it would then accelerate from *subsonic* speed to three times the speed of sound for a high speed dash across some country where suspicions about war preparations might have been aroused. After several flights like this, an SR-71 would have gathered sufficient information about the suspicious activity. That activity, which might have led one country to attack another, is then determined to be inoffensive by U.S. officials. The United States applies political pressure on the potential attacker and prevents the situation from getting worse. Peace is maintained.

Wearing suits used by the flight crews on the first four NASA Shuttle missions, a pilot and his systems officer walk away from the world's fastest plane.

Early Warning

Planes that daily roam the skies gathering intelligence information do so mainly on the assumption that sudden attacks are not very likely to occur without warning. Surveillance carried out by Lockheed's U-2 and SR-71 planes will gather information over a long period of time, helping provide details about activity going on around the world. But sometimes, sudden attacks do come without any warning at all. Good defense means being ready for the unexpected at all times. It does no good to be ready, though, if the means to react quickly does not exist. Early

Regarded by many as the world's finest AWACS plane, the Boeing E3 Sentry is capable of detecting enemy planes to a distance of 300 miles.

Multi-purpose consoles can be set up for many different tasks the AWACS operators are called upon to perform inside the E3.

warning planes do just that. They help watch for sudden attack and are equipped to warn of it just as quickly.

Airborne Warning and Control System (AWACS) is the term applied to a very special class of airplane. Because they are packed with very sensitive electronic sensors and radar equipment with special devices to relay information to a central location, these planes are very expensive, and few countries can afford them. They provide a useful function by giving a country advance warning of impending attack. How can they do this? They are designed to fly at about 30,000 feet and can "see" many hundreds of miles all around, so they pick up incoming at-tack planes long before they arrive.

Radio waves usually travel in straight lines, like light entering the human eye. Standing on the ground, a person can see less than 20 miles in any direction, even if there is no obstruction all the way to the horizon. Yet, at 30,000 feet, an AWACS plane can "see" 237 miles because it is so high. Even if a plane is traveling fast and close to the ground, the AWACS will see it up 30 minutes before it flies by and warn defense fighters to be on the ready. The only alternative to this early warning capability would be to build a tower 30,000 feet high. But even then it would not be as useful, because AWACS planes can be fanned out several hundred miles on the

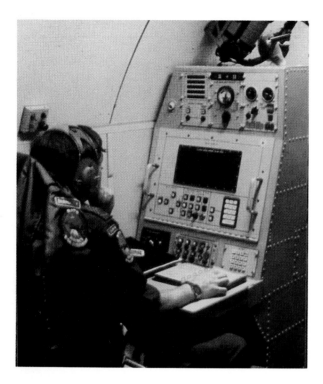

With a flight crew of four, and thirteen systems officers monitoring intelligence information coming in from a wide area, AWACS planes may give the first warning of attack should it come by surprise.

The Sentry usually has a flight crew of four with thirteen people monitoring the consoles and maintaining equipment that provides information on what the radar picks up. The full area surveyed is divided into as many as 24 separate sectors like so many slices in a pie. Each sector looks at a specific aspect of the objects detected. For instance, one sector of the rotating beam will measure position and range as it sweeps past. The next pie-slice in the beam will measure height, a third will look for ships on the sea, and a fourth might combine the first and third to provide location and distance of moving vessels. As the various sections of the radar beam rotate past the objects in question, a picture is built up. When all this information is brought together, or converged, it builds up a three dimensional picture of the skies around and the sea below.

The U.S. Air Force has bought almost 40 Sentry planes. Many of these operate overseas in support of NATO, the North Atlantic Treaty Organization. NATO is made up of the United States, Canada, Iceland, Great Britain, and eleven other countries united in a defensive screen against surprise attack. It was formed in 1949, and Sentry has an important job standing guard on the outpost of that alliance.

edge of a defensive circle around the country they are protecting. This way they can provide a lot more warning time.

The most successful AWACS plane today is the Boeing E3 Sentry. It was developed in the late 1960s, but various modifications have kept it ahead of the competition ever since. It was based on the Boeing 707 airliner and carries a strange-looking dome on top, 30 feet in diameter and 6 feet thick. Set up on two 11-foot tall pedestals, it covers two D-shaped radar antennas that constantly revolve to keep the bearings lubricated. On station, scanning for enemy planes, the dome makes one full revolution every 6 seconds, sending out a beam like a searchlight. Unlike a searchlight, the beam cannot be seen. Nodding up and down as it slowly rotates, the beam sweeps a portion of the sky to a distance of 300 miles. It can monitor everything from ground level up to a height of 80,000 feet.

The heart of the AWACS radar scanning capability is the huge dome fixed by two struts to the top of the plane's body. It rotates in flight to keep the bearing lubricated even when not in use.

Although AWACS planes operate primarily to give early warning of attack, they must also co-ordinate the response from fighters and strike planes rising to counter the threat. Planes like these operate long distances from base and are sometimes refueled in mid-air by tankers.

Scanning the Battle

The most vulnerable seats to be in during a real air war are those belonging to the recon-naissance pilot and his navigator. They fly the roughest, most buffeted, missions of any warplane because they must keep very close to the ground, penetrate deep into enemy airspace, and do it without any defensive weapons to protect themselves. If a real war should break out it might begin in Europe. It is there that the Russians and their allies have an advantage in numbers. It is also the only place United States

Seen over an English countryside, an RF-4 reconnaissance Phantom is escorted by two F-5 fighters in a practice run where pilots will train for a war time surveillance mission.

Infrared imaging from the Phantom's sensors provides a line-scan picture from heat created by the different objects on the ground.

military forces directly face Soviet troops. Because of this, the United States keeps large numbers of flying personnel in NATO bases as part of USAFE, the United States Air Forces Europe.

Training is a vital part of being ready to go into action and, although USAFE reconnaissance crews never trespass across the border, they practice night and day to do so if it ever became necessary. They average about 14 missions, called sorties, every day — all year round. In wartime, that would increase to about 60 a day. In training it takes about four hours to set up a mission, plan the route and decide when to use which cameras for what. In wartime, that would be compressed to one hour at most for a mission lasting one hour in the air.

A typical wartime mission into enemy airspace would begin with the briefing at,

perhaps, a forward air base in West Germany. On the runway stand six McDonnell Douglas RF-4 Phantom fighters carrying a range of different cameras instead of guns or rockets. The briefing over, pilots and navigation officers run to their planes, clutching detailed maps of the route and computer control tapes made up for their specific mission. They will plug those into cassettes in the cockpit to give them continuous displays projected up on the windscreens, showing the way through enemy defenses. In the air, the six planes form up and head off at an altitude of 2,000 feet for enemy territory. They will enter it at the place known simply as the FEBA, the Forward Edge of the Battle Area. Long before then they drop to an altitude of just 250 feet.

On their way to the FEBA the six Phantoms are controlled through dense airspace, like

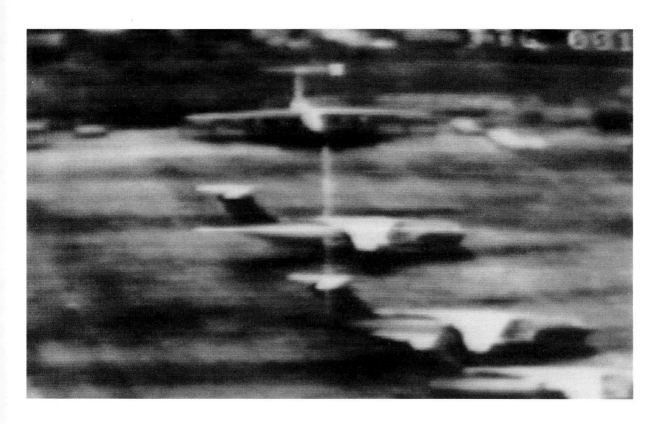

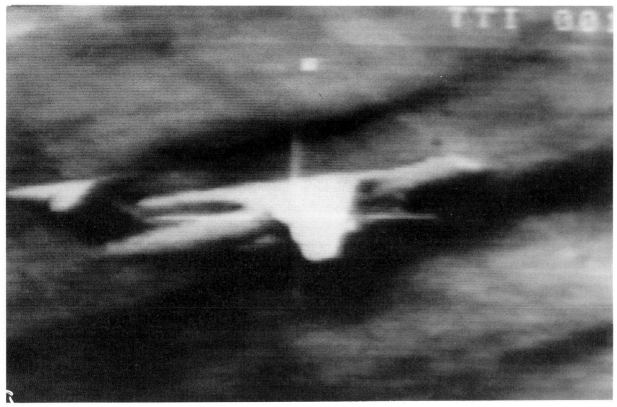

24

Reconnaissance pictures are sometimes taken as strike missions are taking place. In this amazing shot a Pave Tack imaging system is targeting Soviet transport planes on the ground at Tripoli Airport during an Air Force strike in April 1986.

Taken literally one second from the time the attacking F-111 flies over the target, this Soviet aircraft will receive a direct hit where the crossed lines meet.

airliners at a major airport. If they are lucky they will get fighter escort to fend off waves of attacking intruders. Most times they will not because the fighters are themselves trying to gain control of the air. Guided on complex paths around packs of enemy planes hunting for unprotected victims, the Phantoms fly precisely at their allotted height. Above them, fighter-bombers struggle back from the battle zone. Higher still, outgoing heavy attack planes thunder past going toward the enemy at the speed of sound. Below them all, less than 200 feet above the ground, helicopters swarm back and forth bringing wounded to hospitals and carrying troops to the front line. If they are very unlucky they will batter their way through helicopter gunships blasting an advancing col-

umn of enemy tanks. Not a place to linger.

Close to the FEBA, the Phantoms separate and spread out. Now there will be no chance of protection from friendly fighters. Higher flying escort planes would simply draw attention to the unarmed reconnaissance aircraft. They cross the enemy lines at 250 feet, and stay at that height until they return, perhaps thirty minutes later. Using a special pod called Pave Tack mounted below the fuselage, the crew get a long range, infrared, scan of the target area miles ahead. They will fly through the heat of defensive gunfire and anti-aircraft missiles at 550 MPH, slow enough to make it a rough, uncomfortable ride. With no weapons to shoot back, sensors and cameras are set in motion for a low pass over the target area. The dash back to base will carry them through any number of near collisions, and through the full heat of a raging land battle under smoke, fire, and perhaps rain and low cloud. Back at base, those that returned will have intelligence information in the hands of their battle commanders within 45 minutes of wheels stop.

This clear view of a Pave Tack surveillance pod shows how it would be set up for a deep strike mission using an F-15E Strike Eagle.

Filling the Gaps

Information gathered by reconnaissance planes in wartime can make all the difference between winning or losing. In peacetime, satellites are used to keep watch on the way potentially hostile countries are building up their armies or moving their missile bases around. In war, however, the speed of combat would make satellites useless for this task. Satellites take at least 90 minutes to go around the earth once. Because the earth spins on its axis, it can be many hours before a satellite comes back over the same place. Planes are the only means of peering behind enemy defenses to gather detailed information about troop movements and battle formations.

The fast interpretation of information is extremely important to the troops on the ground. Their commanders can only act properly upon receiving good intelligence information. Much attention, therefore, has gone into training both the flight crews and the people on the ground who process photographs and interpret the pictures. Getting the film back to earth is very important. USAFE flight crews train regularly in Europe because weather and the terrain conditions there are very different from those in the United States.

Reconnaissance crews cannot realistically simulate low-flying conditions in the United States because airplanes are prohibited from flying below 500 feet. No such restriction exists in Europe, and there are some places where planes are allowed to get down as low as they can. Accordingly, to train for any sort of low-altitude reconnaissance mission in any part of the world, Europe is the best place to rehearse. USAFE crews are sent to bases in Europe for about two years. They return to the United States with knowledge about flying conditions, bad weather, and even the layout of the towns and villages. That sort of information would be very useful if reconnaissance units in Europe had to be reinforced during a potential war. Those same crews would go back and quickly regain familiarity with their surroundings.

Film processing is carried out in a special building protected from blast and the effects of bombs landing close by. Several mobile vans are available to leave the site and take cover in woods or forests while carrying on the job of processing film from the reconnaissance planes. When a film canister arrives, it is tagged with

Landing back at base, an RF-4 reconnaissance Phantom returns with film canisters full of valuable information. Note the bulging camera section under the nose and the black side window.

Film from the camera's canisters is fed into special machines when it has been processed, tagged with the location it was shot and prepared for interpretation.

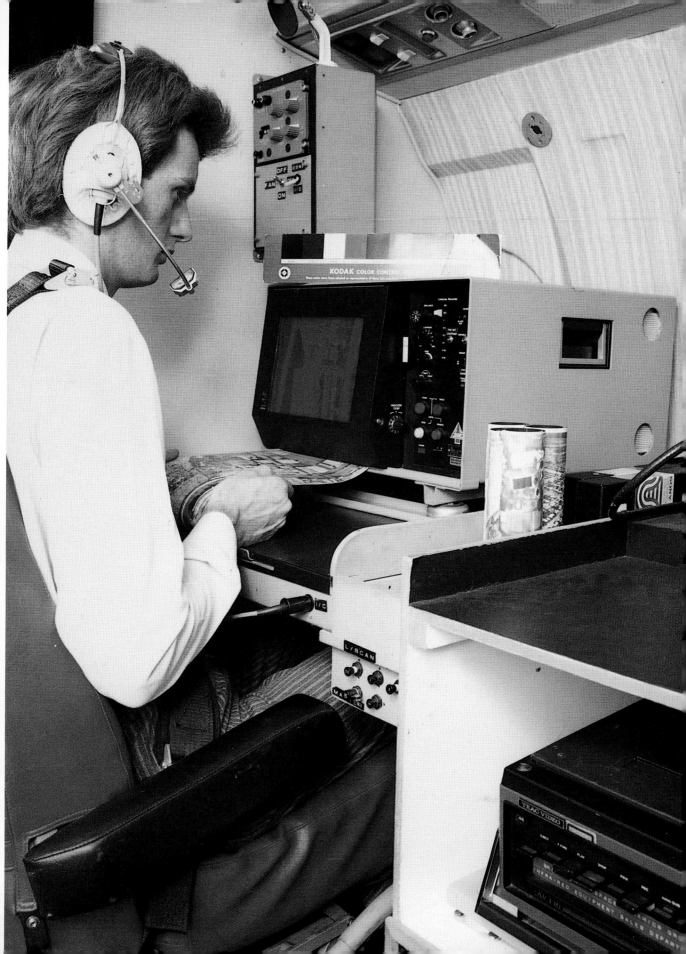

information about the camera system it was used in, the name of the crew, details about the plane and information on time and location where it was shot. The film is processed automatically and then goes to a special interpretation facility where it is analyzed.

Loaded with coded information about landmarks such as bridges, buildings, and rivers, a computer scans the film to identify the precise location from pre-arranged maps. This speeds the process of locating to within a few hundred feet the exact area where the film was shot. Using a standard report form, personnel check off activity within the picture using very high-powered magnifiers. This provides information from which intelligence officers put together a report about men and material within the picture frame being examined. They will fill in a standard set of questions, such as ''How many tanks can you see?'', ''Are there helicopters on the ground?'', or ''Can you identify any crashed planes?''

Many different groups anxiously await information brought back by the reconnaissance planes. Army units want to know what is likely to be the threat they face in the next several hours. Troop positions will be reorganized according to

This view of the Benina Airfield in Libya taken by an SR-71 is typical of the kind of picture returned by a fast flying surveillance plane.

1. Flood Lights
2 Full Oil Tanks
3. Possible Aviation Fuel
4. Street Lights
5. MT Area
6. Bowser Area

This shot is taken by an infrared line-scan camera and shows detailed objects around a local airport.

what the camera sees, and air strikes will be made based on where the enemy is posing the greatest likelihood of a breakthrough. This information is eventually fed back to the air units, who can then avoid heavy concentrations of enemy ground troops and reach their own targets deep behind the front line of battle.

Reconnaissance pilots and their crew members often provide the vital information important to the safety of defense forces and the success of military operations.

Protecting the Navy

One of the most vulnerable, yet valuable, assets in the United States navy is the unique carrier battle group capable of projecting United States defense forces to any place on earth.

Like the U.S. Air Force, the U.S. Navy operates its own *airborne early warning* (AEW) system, not as visible but just as important for national defense as the more elaborate land-based network. Protecting the fleet in times of national crisis or war depends upon good intelligence. That, in turn, means that the fleet must be kept informed of potential threats from land, sea, or air. The national intelligence agencies based in the United States report important information to the carrier battle groups, large groups of ships comprised of one or more aircraft carriers, frigates, destroyers and submarines. However, events far away at sea happen too quickly to depend solely on advanced warning from land. So the carriers themselves must receive information from aircraft they carry for early warning.

Just as submarines listen for sounds of approaching enemy ships or other submarines, so do airborne early warning planes keep the ships informed of threats from the air. Because so many naval operations are carried out cooperatively with other U.S. air and, sometimes, ground forces, naval AEW is vital for a proper response to hostility.

Seen from high above, a typical carrier battle group at sea forms a distorted X-shape with the carrier at the center. The corners of the X form a square 50 miles on each side, covering a surface area of 250 square miles. Flanking the carrier, two cruisers form an inner defense shield for the floating air base. Eight miles ahead, fanned out to either side, two more cruisers weave a watching pattern over the sea to guard approach lanes. Right out in front, perhaps 35 miles distant from the carrier and 50 miles apart, two high-speed destroyers guard the leading edge of the battle group.

To the rear, an equal distance from the carrier, two frigates scan the skies for air attack.

Closer in, between the frigates and the carrier, two destroyers help protect the rear. Beneath the waves, silently tracking back and forth, a mix of submarines sweeps the ocean for signs of enemy vessels. In all, the battle group consists of up to fifteen ships (including submarines), one hundred planes and more than 12,000 men, and its total firepower equals that of all the forces deployed in the Second World War.

If the battle group is within 1,550 miles of

Vessels like this Soviet Oscar class nuclear-powered cruise missile submarine, would pose a serious threat to the carrier battle group in war time. Naval surveillance forces work ceaselessly to maintain a watch on where these ships are located.

Lockheed's S-3B Viking here seen with Harpoon anti-shipping missiles would be a vital part of anti-submarine warfare, searching and eventually destroying the undersea threat to carrier battle groups.

land, it might be able to use the Lockheed P-3 Orion, capable of flying that far and staying above the carrier force for up to three hours before returning home. The Orion can provide warning of enemy submarines by roaming beyond the range of carrier based planes and searching the sea with special electronic probes. Backing up the Orion, the carrier's Lockheed S-3 Viking carries some of the most advanced electronic monitoring equipment for anti-submarine warfare. Like the Orion, it can attack submarines with topedoes, bombs, or mines. For true AEW and AWACS duty against airborne threats, the Grumman E-2 Hawkeye watches over the battle group.

Designed with a unique arrangement of four fins and rudders to make room for a large streamlined *fairing* over the radar antenna, Hawkeye can watch activity up to 500 miles away. Loitering at a height of 30,000 feet for six hours, it can track 250 separate objects and control 30 airborne interceptions, all at the same time, coordinating fighters and attack planes from the carrier as well as shore bases. Hawkeye carries two pilots and three specialists watching instruments and displays from more than 30 advanced electronic monitoring devices.

Tiny cruise missiles can be tracked at a range of up to 120 miles, fighter planes at 230 miles, and bombers at 289 miles. Each carrier has only four Hawkeyes but they are the most valued and maintained planes in the fleet.

Built by Grumman, the E-2C Hawkeye naval surveillance and tracking plane is used to watch activity up to 500 miles away at sea.

Three specialists inside the Hawkeye surveillance plane watch instruments and displays to monitor airborne activity nearly 300 miles away.

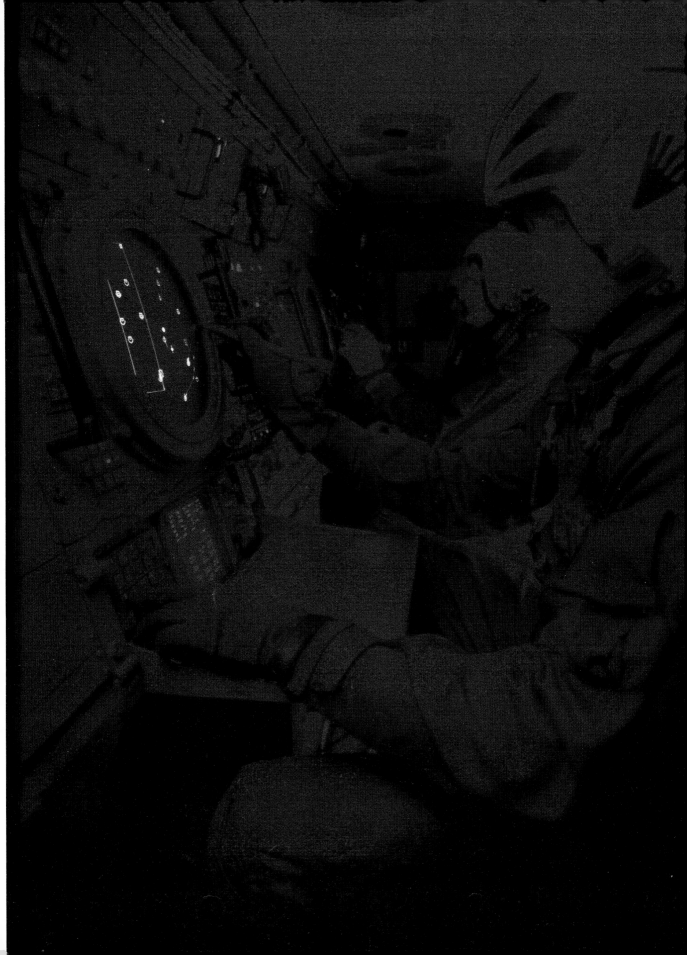

Beating
the Threat

At sea the navy needs protection from surface and subsurface threats, as well as from fast-flying planes bringing cruise missiles or *stand-off* bombs to attack the aircraft carriers and their escort ships. The battle group also needs good intelligence information to handle surface and subsurface threats on its own or with the aid of patrolling airplanes. The same information is also of use to military planners who watch for activity in the world's oceans that might threaten the interests of the United States.

Surface vessels cruising through international waters are easy to follow. Satellites keep a constant vigil on shipping that moves in and out of various ports in certain countries, planes track and record their passage from one place to another, and regular reports from friendly air and naval forces helps log the vessels in and out

Threats to United States ships at sea may come from a variety of weapons, one of the most threatening being stand-off cruise missiles released from bombers several hundred miles over the horizon.

Strategic missiles launching submarines like this Soviet Typhoon class vessel could deliver a near crippling blow to land based missiles or bombers from their position just off the coast.

of different regions. Subsurface vessels are a different matter. They are quiet and spend most of their time submerged. Some submarines pose the greatest threat possible, because they are designed for one purpose only: to go as deep as possible in remote areas of the world's oceans. These particular submarines carry large numbers of nuclear-tipped missiles, each capable of destroying several cities.

About one-third of United States *strategic nuclear warheads* are kept in submarines capable of escaping a surprise attack that might knock out land-based missiles or bombers before they could get off the ground. This gives assurance that a sudden missile strike on United

States territory would never destroy all of the defense forces. A third are at sea, safely hidden under the waves. The ability of these submarines to avoid attack by remaining hidden, their whereabouts unknown, is crucial to convincing a potential aggressor that attack is not worth the risk of his own destruction.

Lockheed's S-3A Viking (top left) and P-3 Orion patrol for the U.S. Navy on extended anti-submarine duties protecting the surface fleet.

Also hidden in the world's oceans are British, French, Russian, and Chinese submarines with nuclear missiles on board. The United States works to keep track of those submarines and at the same time keep its own submarines hidden. Several types of planes are given the job of spying on these subsurface threats in the hope of tracking them and finding out where they hide. Satellites watch as they slip away from home ports, and patrolling Navy planes observe them as they cruise through shallow water. Tracking a submerged submarine is very difficult, so every effort goes into keeping it in view as long as possible.

The Orion is equipped with complex and sophisticated sensors to detect submarines and carries weapons capable of destroying them if they are recognized to be hostile.

Special planes like the Lockheed P-3 Orion and the S-3 Viking are only part of the answer. They need effective sensors and special equipment to help them detect these submarines at depth. The sonar detectors used to pick up sound transmitted through the water are only effective if operators know the temperature and the salinity (the amount of salt) in the sea. These factors affect the nature of the signals coming back. To measure them, the Orion drops a device called a bathy-thermograph into the ocean. This device unreels a long wire which slowly lowers a sensor to measure temperature and salinity. The information is transmitted to the plane overhead and used to help interpret sonar signal equipment.

Cruise missiles fired from the torpedo tubes of submerged submarines pose a serious threat.

Before they surface and rise into the air, cruise missiles are shaped like torpedoes. Then small wings pop out and carry the missiles to their targets, which can be several miles inland. Good intelligence information can provide details about the intentions of a potential enemy in war, allowing time for a defense to be planned and put into action. Anti-cruise missile systems are able to rely on good intelligence gathered during peacetime to provide the knowledge that helps deal with the new threat.

A very serious threat to surface shipping exists from submarines launching cruise missiles that once surfaced deploy wings and rocket motors to fly swiftly to their targets.

Electronic Probes

Surprise attack has always been a threat countries live under. Many times, dictators and unwise rulers have gambled that by trying to overwhelm the opposition in one fatal blow, they will win a war. One of the worst forms of sudden attack is called *blitzkreig,* a violent form of combat in which an aggressor seeks to crush an opposing force by massed assault using tanks, guns, and planes. Blitzkreig was used by Adolph Hitler when he attacked Poland in 1939 and started the Second World War that raged until 1945. In today's technological environment, blitzkreig can be considerably worse, terrifying by nature and devastating in its impact on people and towns.

Because electronic controls and radar play an important part in all forms of warfare, it is important to jam the enemy's signals as effectively as possible. The radar sets and electronic sensors used to detect the presence of the opposition are an enemy's eyes and ears. Without them, he is unable to attack with ferocity or purpose, because he cannot know where the opposing forces are located. To wage a successful blitzkreig assault, a country needs tight

The effective jamming of enemy signals would be important in any war, not least during a sudden "blitzkrieg" attack like that depicted here as Soviet tanks move rapidly through country roads.

One of the most effective ways of protecting defending airplanes is to shield them from electronic detection by special jamming planes carrying sensors like this on an EF-111 Raven.

control of its attacking forces. If the eyes and ears of the forces are impaired, the enemy is virtually blind.

One way of impairing the enemy is to place an electronic shroud over enemy radar and sophisticated sensors. Called *countermeasures*, this action counters the attempt to electronically illuminate the presence of men, equipment, and machines. Countermeasures have a two-fold purpose: they can help to stop the effectiveness of a blitzkreig attack and they can hide the military forces brought up to stop the assault. Aircraft that jam, spread clutter, or otherwise distort the enemy's radar equipment are engaged in electronic countermeasures. Planes that veil the presence of attacking forces in response to blitzkreig are said to be *force multipliers*, because they help fighters and bombers survive longer as though there were many more aircraft involved. They provide an invisible tunnel,

Converted by Grumman from a General Dynamics F-111 fighter bomber, the Raven would provide an electronic cloak to hide the rapid movement of fighters and interceptors sent up to counter an unprovoked attack.

within which aircraft follow behind, undetected and free to go about their business in enemy airspace.

One of the most effective force multipliers is the Grumman EF-111A, dubbed the Electronic Fox. More formally called the Raven, this plane is developed from the very successful General Dynamics F-111 fighter-bomber. Its job is to confuse, shroud, and eliminate the ability of enemy radar sets to see incoming attack planes. In this way, under the awesome and overwhelming superiority of a blitzkreig assault, the Raven would clear a path for low-flying battlefield attack planes. Entering the path might be F-15 Strike Eagles flying low and fast to drop anti-tank weapons, or the F-111 fighter-bomber capable of deep penetration of enemy airspace.

One plane sent out in force to halt the tanks would be the robust and highly survivable Fairchild A-10 Thunderbolt. Arguably one of the

ugliest planes around, the Thunderbolt is not built for speed. It lopes along at 250 to 350 MPH but, with a powerful General Electric Gatling gun in the nose, it can blast tanks to pieces with a massive round of cannon shells each the size of a milk bottle. Each shell is made from a form of uranium, the densest of the elements, and leaves the gun muzzle at a speed of 2,400 MPH. By opening a path for strike planes to hit deep behind enemy lines at the source of the blitzkreig, planes like the Thunderbolt can pick off the waves of advancing tanks unmolested from attacking fighters. Their airfields will probably have been destroyed by Strike Eagles and F-111s.

The Raven is capable of a maximum speed of 1,160 MPH, although during a penetration mission it would cruise at 570 MPH. It has a range in excess of 2,000 miles and is packed with electonic jamming equipment. Although not strictly a spy plane, it prevents the detection of friendly planes by enemy radar systems and, as such, can be said to be the world's most efficient anti-spy device.

With enormous fire power greater than anything in the sky today, the gattling gun on this A-10 makes a devastating strike on armored tank columns.

The A-10 Thunderbolt equipped with extensive anti-armor rockets and bombs would be sent out to help deter sudden strike by tank forces, aircraft that would themselves gain the benefit of an electronic shield.

Watching Eyes

When electronic jammers help battles to be won on the ground it is because planes with countermeasures have gone ahead of the responding force to shield it from detection. So it has to be in the hostile environment of a carrier-launched attack. Two vital jobs help ensure the safety of strike planes waiting to go off a carrier deck. The first job is to provide the background intelligence information that enables mission-planning officers to decide which planes should go where during the strike. The second job is to help keep the planes veiled from the prying eyes of enemy radar and electronic sensors.

A typical aircraft carrier equipped with more than 80 planes includes two squadrons of the most potent naval multi-role fighter anywhere in the world. Built by Grumman, the F-14 Tomcat has *variable-geometry* swing wings enabling it to

Equipped with a TARPS reconnaissance pod, this F-14 Tomcat makes a tight turn before a surveillance run over hostile territory.

Large planes carry surveillance crews and here specialists in an E-6A Tacamo aircraft scan potentially hostile air space for incoming fighters and attack bombers.

fly very fast and turn quickly or slowly for low-speed maneuverability. It exists to protect the outer defenses of the carrier battle group, involving many planes and ships. In one squadron, each with 12 planes, three Tomcats are there for a very different job. Usually fitted with an array of anti-aircraft missiles, one version strips away its offensive armament for a special pack of scanning instruments.

This special pack called the Tactical Airborne Reconnaissance Pod System, or TARPS, has been developed for reconnaissance duty over great distances. The pod carries panoramic cameras to give wide-angle views from one horizon to the other, special infrared scanners to build up heat maps of the ground below, and a serial-frame camera for special shots of specific objects. TARPS has a control system to keep its temperature within certain limits and control equipment linked to the left operator's console in the back seat of the Tomcat.

TARPS-equipped Tomcats have performed many functions in support of general intelligence-gathering duties and have put together maps of hostile ground forces for use by carrier strike planes going in to attack. With reconnaissance

Without protection, naval forces would suffer direct strike but, even with today's rugged ships, would result in significant loss of life.

Grumman's EA6 Prowler is a converted electronic countermeasures plane, based on the A-6 Intruder, many of which it would be sent ahead of to protect against detection by enemy radar as they neared their intended targets.

to help them decide where to send the attack planes. As soon as those planes leave the carrier and depart the protected haven of the carrier's own defenses, they can be on their own in a very hostile, enemy-occupied place. A specially modified version of the A-6 Intruder, a part of the carrier's medium attack force, has been developed into the EA-6 Prowler. This plane has been built as a tactical electronic warfare plane. Its job is to fly comparatively slow and place a veil over the enemy's radar.

The Prowler has extra space and seats for two additional crew members, accommodating four in all. On top of the tail it carries a bulbous fairing over receivers that collect enemy radar transmissions. Under the wings, it has high-powered jamming transmitters operated by computers behind the two cockpits. Prowlers can be refueled in flight, perhaps before they rendezvous with Intruders flying in from the carrier to follow the jamming plane through enemy airspace. The Prowler must remain with the strike planes until the last one has left enemy territory, scrambling signals and communications until the attack force has returned. The Prowler can fly 2,400 miles on internal fuel and usually flies at around 620 MPH. It is the passport to a two-way ticket for pilots that ride under its electronic veil.

pack in place, Tomcats have been used extensively in the Mediterranean Sea from carriers patrolling near the Lebanese city of Beirut. On more than one occasion, they have made low-level flights over Beirut's densely populated district to gather pictures of buildings where hostages were believed to be kept. This duty is not as dramatic as flying directly in support of defensive action, but it draws the same amount of gunfire from the ground and is just as important.

When Tomcats with TARPS gather mapping details and general reconnaissance intelligence, mission planners sometimes use the information

The Prowler is designed to go low and fast to jam radars, detect unknown threats, and generally provide a screen through which the carrier attack planes can do their job.

ABBREVIATIONS

AAM	Air-To-Air Missile
AEW	Airborne Early Warning
AWACS	Airborne Warning and Control System
FEBA	Forward Edge of the Battle Area
NATO	North Atlantic Treaty Organization
TARPS	Tactical Airborne Reconnaissance Pod System
USAFE	United States Air Forces in Europe

GLOSSARY

Arc

Part of the circumference of a circle or other curve.

Blitzkrieg

A fighting technique that takes its name literally from the German name for thunder and lightning war, this term implies massive armored attack at high speed using a great deal of force.

Countermeasures

In electronic warfare, any passive or active equipment designed to confuse or disturb radio signals broadcast from a transmitter with the object of detecting solid bodies. Basically, devices or equipment installed to help the carrier (such as a plane, ship, or tank) avoid detection.

Fairing

The smoothing of two angular surfaces so there is a blended contour between the two.

Force multipliers

Some way in which a weapon system can be made much more effective in a manner equivalent to providing more of the same but in fact getting that kind of improvement from greatly improved efficiency.

Infrared

The part of the electromagnetic spectrum with a longer wavelength than light but a shorter wavelength than radio waves. Like radio waves, infrared radiation cannot be seen with the unaided human eye.

Mach

Mach 1, or unity, is the speed of sound: 760 MPH at sea level, decreasing to 660 MPH at a height of 36,000 feet. Mach 2.2 is equivalent to a speed of 1,672 MPH at sea level or 1,452 MPH above 36,000 feet.

Stand-off

In the context of a weapon, one that has its own propulsion which when released can transport a warhead to a target some distance away from the carrier-plane.

Strategic nuclear warheads

Defined as nuclear devices delivered by long range planes or missiles across distances of intercontinental range. That is, a nuclear missile capable of flying between, for instance, the United States and another continent. The Soviet Union deems a strategic weapon to be any weapon capable of striking Soviet territory.

Subsonic

Any speed below the speed of sound, which is about 760 MPH at sea level or about 660 MPH at 36,000 feet and above.

Variable-geometry

A means by which the shape of an airplane wing can be changed in flight by attaching the wing to a pivot where it joins the main body (fuselage) so it can be swiveled to any position. This wing design is also called the swing-wing.

INDEX

Page references in *italics* indicate photographs or illustrations.